© 2003 by Adam Jones, Steve Kemp, and Tide-mark Press
Published by Tide-mark Press, Ltd.
P.O. Box 20, Windsor, CT 06095-0020

Printed and bound in Korea by Samhwa Printing Co.
Book design: Evelyn Dombkowski
Cover design: Dan Veale

Library of Congress Cataloging-in-Publication Data

Jones, Adam and Kemp, Steve
Great Smoky Mountains: Natural Wonder, National Park
82 p. cm.

ISBN 1-55949-743-2 Hardcover Edition

Library of Congress Control Number
2003113660

GREAT SMOKY MOUNTAINS

Natural Wonder, National Park

Photographs by Adam Jones   Text by Steve Kemp

Tide-mark Press

Windsor, Connecticut

IN THE MOUNTAINS

This scene at sunrise from Clingmans Dome appears like an ocean of mountain ridges and valleys. At 6,643 feet, Clingmans Dome is the highest point in Great Smoky Mountains National Park. An observation tower provides magnificent views from this summit.

There are stately groves of virgin forest with towering hemlock trees that were saplings when Columbus set sail for the New World. There are wildflowers of every conceivable hue that decorate the land from deepest hollow to highest ridge. In summer, fawns bound across green fields and black bears lumber beside splashy mountain streams. Yet, above all, it is mountains that lure people to America's most popular national park. It is the first sight of the distant, blue, beautiful Great Smoky Mountains that vacationers imagine as they pack their cars and depart from Atlanta and Louisville, Cincinnati and Birmingham.

That we regard mountains as lovely is an all but universal truth. Simply gazing upon mountains from a roadside overlook or the front porch of an inn raises our spirits. Mountains are where we go to find sanctuary apart from our everyday lives. In *Our National Parks,* John Muir put it this way, "Climb the mountains and get their good tidings. Nature's peace will flow into you as sunshine flows into trees. The winds will blow their own freshness into you, and the storms their energy, while cares will drop off like autumn leaves."

As mountain ranges go, the Great Smokies are neither America's highest nor most majestic. There are no sheer granite walls or icy spires like those that epitomize the Rockies or Sierras. But many who know the Smokies will insist that these ancient highlands are America's most beautiful mountain range. The Great Smokies are welcoming rather than menacing. They comfort more than they challenge. To traipse a winding path through a rich cove hardwood forest beside a mossy mountain stream is to feel at home, even if you have never visited the Smoky Mountains before.

Even the skyline of the Smokies is somehow human in form. Backlit by a setting sun, the ridges are rounded and sensual, like the bare curves of the human body. No summits rise above timberline--all are warmly cloaked in forests and flowers. Life is everywhere abundant, and incredibly diverse.

Age is the power that has gentled these mountains. The Smokies are part of the Appalachian Range that reaches from northern Alabama to Quebec and is one of the oldest existing mountain ranges on the planet. The Appalachians (including the Smokies) were uplifted 200 to 300 million years ago, and consequently have been exposed to eons of relentless weathering. At one time the highlands of the Smokies probably stood as tall as today's Rockies, but their summits have been reduced by ice, wind, and water, creating terrain more hospitable to woodlands and wildlife.

The rock that is the backbone of the Smokies is older than the mountains themselves. Along the eastern edge of the Smokies, near Bryson City, North Carolina, geologists have found rock over one billion years old. Since this rock pre-dates hard-bodied life on earth, it contains no fossils. Other rocks were formed 450 to 550 million years ago when trilobites and toothed worms called conodonts inhabited the seas. Fossilized bits of these creatures can occasionally be found in Cades Cove and on Chilhowee Mountain.

Nearly all the rock in the park is sedimentary, formed by deposits of sand, soil, and gravel washed into shallow seas from the surrounding uplands. Over millions of years these materials became cemented

The forest canopy, seen here in spring, occupies the highest part of the woodland ecosystem. The canopy receives the majority of sunlight and rain that falls on the forest. By controlling the air space above, trees influence growth on the floor of the forest below.

Peaks of greening mountain slopes stretch to the horizon along the southern Appalachian Mountains. This view in North Carolina is typical of the Blue Ridge Parkway, what many people consider America's most scenic drive. The Parkway follows mountaintops from Virginia's Shenandoah National Park to the more-than-500,000-acre Great Smoky Mountains National Park in North Carolina and Tennessee.

A snow-covered mountain slope at Newfound Gap reflects the winter sun. The Tennessee-North Carolina border and the Appalachian Trail cross Newfound Gap from east to west. Discovered in the 19th century, Newfound Gap is the lowest drivable pass through the Smokies. It replaced Indian Gap, the original route two miles to the west traveled by the Cherokees.

into layers of rock over nine miles thick. Today, these rocks bear the names of Smoky Mountain landmarks: Thunderhead Sandstone (Thunderhead Mountain), Anakeesta (Anakeesta Ridge), Elkmont Sandstone (Elkmont Logging Camp), Roaring Fork Sandstone (Roaring Fork), and Metcalf Phyllite (Metcalf Bottoms).

Though less than half as high as the Rockies, the Smokies are of respectable stature relative to other mountains east of the Mississippi River. At 6,643 feet, Clingmans Dome, the highest peak in the Smokies, is the third highest summit in the East. Twelve mountains in the Smokies exceed 6,000 feet in elevation. Mt. Le Conte, if measured from its base near Gatlinburg, Tennessee, to its zenith at High Top, earns a base-to-summit height of 5,301 feet, better than any other eastern mountain and rivaling many Rocky Mountain peaks.

Great Smoky Mountains National Park straddles the border between Tennessee and North Carolina, well south of the Mason-Dixon line. For Southerners in particular, part of the lure of mountains is the cool relief they offer in summer. As you climb in elevation, air pressure decreases and air expands. You may have noted this by the way your water bottle or packaged food bulges when you drive into the mountains. More widely spaced air molecules equal cooler temperatures. In general, for every 1,000 feet you gain in elevation, the temperature drops about three degrees Fahrenheit. Consequently, atop Mt. Guyot or Clingmans Dome, the weather may be a delightful 15 to 20 degrees cooler than in nearby Knoxville, Tennessee.

In fact, at Le Conte Lodge, a rustic resort near the top of Mt. Le Conte, employees claim the temperature has never reached 80 degrees Fahrenheit, even though the neighboring lowlands, not two airline miles distant, swelter in the upper 80s and 90s all summer long. The first frost sometimes touches Clingmans Dome in August, and by the end of October, snow has usually dusted the peaks a time or two. In April or even May, late snowstorms regularly close the Newfound Gap Road, the main thoroughfare across the mountain range.

The effects of elevation can be compared to latitude and seasons as well. Geographers have calculated that gaining 1,000 feet in elevation is the equivalent to traveling 330 miles north. Spring is said to advance up the mountains at a pace of 100 vertical feet per day. Likewise, in September, autumn and its changing foliage descend from the summits at the same rate.

In the not-so-distant days before air conditioning, escaping to the cool comfort of the mountains was even more appealing than it is today. Asheville, North Carolina, home of the massive Grove Park Inn and Vanderbilt mansion, provided tony summering grounds for those with the means to leave behind the soggy heat and yellow fever of the Southeastern coastal plains. Health spas, retreats, and comfortable resorts dotted the foothills of the southern mountains in Maryville and Elkmont, Tennessee; and Highlands, Balsam Mountain, and Black Mountain, North Carolina. Summer afternoons were spent in wicker chairs in the shade of wide porches in anticipation of cool breezes slipping down from the peaks. Nights were even more enjoyable, with the tall windows of the inns flung wide open to welcome the brisk air and the sounds of katydids and crickets.

Besides temperature, the Great Smoky Mountains profoundly affect weather in another way: precipitation. Moisture-laden air frequently approaches the Smokies from the south and the west, from the Gulf of Mexico and the Pacific. Weather systems must rise over the peaks of the Smokies to gain passage, and as moist air rises it automatically cools and condenses, shedding some of its load in the form of rain, sleet, or snow. Along the high crests of the Smokies, an average of 88 inches of rain falls annually. During a wet year, over eight feet of water will drench the high country.

Hiking along Porters Creek or Goshen Prong, or any of the other steeper drainages, signs of flash floods are everywhere. After an explosive summer thunderstorm, or a prolonged winter downpour, literal walls of water crash down the mountainsides carrying logs, root balls, rocks, and other debris. Gullies 20 feet deep, gouged during a single cloudburst, are visible from the Alum Cave Trail. Along most any stream, great tangles of sun-bleached timber mark where a flood surge deposited it load. Every year or two a hiker misjudges the force and depth of a rain-swollen stream and is swept to his death while attempting a crossing.

All of this precipitation is also the reason for the metaphorical "smoke" for which the Smokies are named. As the skies lift after a storm, streamers of smoke-like clouds slowly twist and swirl from the hollows and drape themselves across the faces of mountain peaks. Hour after hour the mist rises and curls, catching the light and transforming the scenery with each passing moment.

In summer, an ethereal blue haze softens the mountains. This vapor, evaporated from earth and forest, was called "shaconage" (blue, like smoke) by the Cherokee, and it, too, is the smoke for which the mountains are named. Shaconage, a product of water and organic chemicals transpired from the forests, paints distant ridges blue and melts clouds and mountains together at the most distant horizon.

Snowfalls substantial enough to accumulate on the ground occur only three or four times per year in the lowlands, but in the mountains, snow is a common winter visitor. Over five feet of snow annually falls at Newfound Gap, causing the main park thoroughfare to be frequently closed or restricted to vehicles with chains. Occasionally, a sopping wet winter storm system will stream out of the Atlantic and absolutely bury the Smokies in snow. This happened in March of 1993, the often-recalled "Storm of the Century," which set records for low barometric pressure and dumped two feet of snow in the Tennessee Valley. In the Smoky Mountains, drifts of seven feet were reported. Army helicopters winched stranded backpackers from Appalachian Trail shelters, and it was nine days before power could be restored to the park's headquarters near Gatlinburg.

News reports of fresh snow in the Smokies always bring waves of visitors from Florida, south Georgia, and other parts of the Deep South. You can see them piling from their cars at Newfound Gap and at Luftee Overlook, building snowmen, tossing snowballs, and tracing snow angels on a mountainside. Like visitors during the rest of the year, they hurry to the Smokies to see miracles that only mountains can reveal.

Wearing early spring foliage, the Smokies are a wildland habitat to some 100 species of native trees. These ancient mountains provide a great variety of habitats and micro-habitats for both plant and animal life.

Silhouetted in the rising sun, the southern Appalachian Mountain range includes the Great Smoky Mountains, which the Cherokee people described as blue, like smoke or "shaconage." Shaconage results from the mix of water and organic chemicals transpired by the region's dense, wet forests.

Allegheny serviceberry (Amelanchier arborea) is an early blooming tree also known as shadbush. This photograph was taken along Thomas Divide, which is named for William Holland Thomas, a Confederate colonel who commanded Cherokee troops and later helped the Cherokees retain rights to the Qualla Boundary or Eastern Cherokee Reservation.

Catawba rhododendron (Rhododendron catawbiense) *splashes color along the southern end of the Blue Ridge Parkway. Common on higher, exposed mountain ridges, this large shrub blooms with magnificent rose or purple flowers in late June.*

*The park is not always a safe haven. Blighted by an infesta-
tion of balsam woolly adelgid, Fraser firs (Abies fraseri),
with their upright cones and blunt needles, are native only
in the southern Appalachians. The majority of mature
Fraser firs in Great Smoky Mountains National Park have
succumbed to infestation by the adelgid.*

*The higher elevations of the Smokies are frequently snow-
covered during the winter months. Greenbrier Pinnacle in
the northern Smokies was one of several places selected for
the reintroduction of Peregrine Falcons in the 1980s.*

From the Blue Ridge Parkway in North Carolina, Nantahala National Forest appears like a green carpet covering the Great Balsam Mountains. Great Smoky Mountains National Park to the northwest and South Carolina to the south border one of several backbone mountain chains, the Great Balsams. Nantahala is the Indian name for "noon day sun."

At sunset, Morton Overlook, near Newfound Gap, reveals a dramatic succession of mountain peaks and valleys.

Wearing winter white, Mt. Le Conte may have been named for conservationist Joseph Le Conte, a founding member of the Sierra Club, or for his older brother, John Le Conte.

Trees coated with rime suggest an otherworldly landscape in this view from Clingmans Dome. Rime is frozen fog that forms on the windward side of mountains. Clingmans Dome was named for Civil War general and North Carolina politician Thomas Lanier Clingman, who first measured the elevation.

A river of fog streams along the treetops of the valley seen from Morton Overlook. Rolling clouds of fog frequently blanket large areas in the Smokies and contribute measurably to overall precipitation in the mountains.

Framed in fall color, Mt. Le Conte rises to 6,593 feet and is the third-highest peak in the Smokies. Rocky outcroppings like Myrtle Point and Cliff Top offer spectacular views from Mt. Le Conte.

Seen here in autumn, Deep Creek Valley is on the south side of Great Smoky Mountains National Park. The Deep Creek Trail was one of the first constructed after the park was established.

Ridges of color extend toward Deep Creek Valley.

In the Smokies, autumn arrives first at the high elevations, with colors ranging from yellow to scarlet to dark purple. The full range of autumn color in the hardwood forests may be seen from about October 15th to the 31st.

This winter view of Sugarlands Valley is beautiful, but also reveals the dramatic weather changes experienced in the park. Sugarlands Valley was named for its plentiful sugar maple trees. Mountain farmers used the sap from these trees to make sugar and syrup.

THE DEEP DARK FOREST

These parallel rows of trees mark the route of an old road through Cades Cove. A six-mile-long valley at the western end of Great Smoky Mountains National Park, Cades Cove is an historic area that now preserves a number of homes and farm buildings from the 19th and early 20th centuries.

If you do not like verdant, mossy, shadowy, thick trunked, evergreen-scented forest, chances are you will not immediately fall in love with the Great Smoky Mountains. Trees blanket the Smokies the way hair covers a black bear's back. There are arbors of every ilk, from Christmas tree firs to spreading magnolias, from seedlings to 200-foot-tall Goliaths, all interdependent and intertwined in a complex, mysterious, and beautiful fastness. To those of us instinctively drawn to the woods, the Smoky Mountains rekindle the excitement of storybook adventures set in places like Pooh's Hundred Acre Wood, Badger's Wild Wood, and Sherwood Forest.

Trees influence everything that lives in the Smokies. Nowhere else do American black bears spend so much time in the trees. Smoky Mountain bears nap in trees, dine in trees, escape danger in trees, seek winter dens in trees, and (sometimes) are born in trees. Watching a young black bear ascend a perfectly vertical tree trunk, one cannot help but be amazed by how effortless it seems. Indeed, some especially long-limbed Smoky Mountain bruins appear ape-like when perched in the upper braches of a tall tree, reaching for buds or acorns or berries.

The variety of tree-borne food, be it insect larvae, serviceberries, or hickory nuts, is one reason Great Smoky Mountains National Park today boasts what is likely the highest density of truly wild black bears in the contiguous United States. Both black cherry and pin cherry trees are common in the Smokies, and few go through a summer season without a visit by a black bear. The national park's 11 varieties of oaks produce acorns that are rich in fat and protein and are best eaten on the twig before they are devoured by wild hogs, deer, or insects on the ground.

While throughout most of their range black bears retreat to hollow logs, caves, or shallow excavations beneath stumps for their winter dens, in the Smokies at least half of the bears seek out cavities in large, live trees. The voids are cozy places created when a large limb is lost in a windstorm or lightning splits a trunk. Many of the trees are old-growth, a quality now mostly unavailable elsewhere in black bear country.

Black bear dens may be 80 feet above the ground. The height offers more security than ground dens, an important concern since bears may spend four months or more curled within. The trees also offer shelter from the wind and rain and a fair amount of insulation against the high country cold.

Remarkably, many cubs are born in these penthouse dens. The potato-sized cubs are blind at birth and all but helpless. While mom mostly dozes, the cubs (one or two, sometimes three) nurse and rapidly grow in their swaying forest tree house.

By April, the family's restlessness can no longer be contained. The bears peer from the safety of their den to the ground far below. For the three-month old cubs, now weighing 10 to 15 pounds, the first step is a perilous one. Few field observations have been recorded, but it is assumed that the cubs use their disproportionately large claws to gingerly back down the vertical trunk to their first touch of terra firma.

In the scattered stands of virgin forest that dot the Great Smoky Mountains, you will see other living things that do not normally live on trees. If you take a hike along the famous Appalachian Trail, or the upper reaches of the Sugarland Mountain or Noland Divide trails, you are sure to see trees growing in

Mountain farmers used wood from the black walnut (Juglans nigra) *for furniture and gunstocks. The nuts of the tree, like this lone example growing in Cades Cove, provided an appetizing source of protein.*

Butterflies and bees love Joe-Pye weed (Eupatorium purpureum)*, named for a Native American medicine man who used the plant to treat ailments such as rheumatism and kidney stones. The brilliant red blossoms of the cardinal flower* (Lobelia cardinalis) *attract hummingbirds. Though this plant contains poisonous alkaloids, Indians used its leaves and roots in the treatment of digestive disorders.*

The crested dwarf iris (Iris cristata) *is the state flower of Tennessee and was named for the Greek goddess of the rainbow. Smaller than the well-known blue flag iris, the crested dwarf blooms in late April and early May.*

trees. Ten-foot-tall red spruce saplings grow along the horizontal limbs of 200-year-old yellow birch trees. Catawba rhododendron shrubs proliferate 50 feet off the ground in the forks of trees, and a huge variety of ferns, mosses, and lichens flourish on deeply furrowed trunks and crooked branches. Trees like the Fraser fir host at least a dozen species of lichen, some of which are found only on Fraser firs.

This epiphytic ("upon plant") lifestyle is possible because the Smoky Mountains are such a damp place. The red spruce growing on the yellow birch cannot develop much of a root system, but it does not need to. Drenching rains and misty clouds are so prevalent in the high country that the plants never lack moisture.

Much like the rainforests of Central and South America, the lush forests of the Smokies have an interesting life zone in their canopy. During summer, viewed from above, the treetops look like fluffy green clouds with billowing mounds and valleys. Warblers and other birds spend much of their time here, building nests, hunting insects, and flitting from branch to branch in this rich ecological stratum where forest meets the sky.

Aided by lightweight scaffolding and special climbing gear, scientists are just now beginning to explore life in the hardwood forest canopy. Their discoveries include a whole world of insects, lichens, mosses, liverworts, and fungi not commonly found in other park habitats. Because energy from the sun is so much more abundant in the treetops than on the forest floor, there is little doubt that their continued research will net even more revelations.

Beneath the forest canopy, sunlight is so diminished that many plants, and the animals that depend

on them, must struggle to survive. The spring wildflowers that attract bees and throngs of nature-loving humans each April actually do most of their growing before the deciduous trees unfurl their leaves and cast their seven-month shadows. Very early bloomers like hepatica and violets are leafed-out and photosynthesizing by the first day of February. Wildflowers that do bloom in summer generally favor open areas like roadsides, or need to be very tall.

Smoky Mountain forests are Paradise found for squirrels. The squirrels hurl themselves from branch to branch and from tree to tree like long-tailed trapeze artists with little use for the ground. Like bears, they find plenty of buds, fruits, insects, bird eggs, and acorns to eat, and use lofty tree cavities for superior shelter.

Red squirrels and northern flying squirrels occupy the park's higher elevations where spruce, fir, and hemlock are common. When hikers encounter red squirrels, the squirrels are usually chattering at them in an extremely agitated manner. The heckling is loud, constant, and seemingly eternal, as anyone who has ever tried to outwait a red squirrel's scolding can attest. This behavior seems a dubious strategy for survival, but it has earned the eight-ounce mammal the nickname "boomer."

Big-eyed, floppy-skinned northern flying squirrels do not technically fly, but they can glide for distances of 100 feet by leaping from a treetop and stretching tight the ample skin between their front and hind legs. Their tails even function as rudders when aloft. Flying squirrels are mostly nocturnal and are more often heard (they make high-pitched squeaks) than seen. They earn their living off lichens, fungus, seeds, insects, and occasionally young birds.

On down the mountain the southern flying squirrel (slightly smaller than the northern) and the gray squirrel (larger than the red) fill the warmer, drier, hardwood-based ecological niche not occupied by their high elevation cousins. Both are abundant in the lowlands, some would say excessively so, as they brazenly invade the attics and crawl spaces of human dwellings. Perfectly wild southern flying squirrels have even been known to stroll into inhabited houses and calmly make themselves at home on the dinner table.

Relatively few predators have great success with squirrels. Once upon a time mountain folk savored squirrel meat, and hunting gray squirrels with .30 caliber "squirrel rifles" was a common activity. Today in the Great Smokies, snakes take more squirrels than human hunters. Amazingly, large black rat snakes can climb trees, muscling their way up roughened bark to feed on young squirrels. Timber rattlesnakes, which grow up to six feet long in the national park, will strike and consume squirrels along the ground. Owls, especially great horned ones, will take the occasional flying squirrel, and sharp-shinned hawks, which are as quick and agile flying through the trees as a sparrow, will efficiently kill adult red and gray squirrels.

Many other mammals depend on trees for refuge. Raccoons famously retreat from hounds (and coyotes) in the arbors. So do, surprisingly, woodchucks. In the Smokies, even gray foxes climb trees.

As they did elsewhere in the East, loggers, farmers, and town builders at one time relieved the Great Smoky Mountains of most of their trees. Most, but not all. At the heads of the rugged hollows, along rocky ridges and remote coves, some 100,000 acres (160 square miles) of virgin forest survived long enough to be protected by the establishment of Great Smoky Mountains National Park in 1934.

These rare ancient forests differ from the park's 80- to 100-year-old second growth woodlands in ways that are both subtle and obvious. From an architect's point of view, a second growth forest is to old-growth what a subdivision of single family homes is to a cathedral. Second growth is dominated by trees of similar age, height, and girth. Old-growth is infinitely more varied, a diverse community of old, gnarled giants, vibrant saplings, and everything in between. There are at least two climax canopies: the towering overstory where tulip trees, northern red oaks, white oaks, basswoods, silver bells, sugar maples, red maples, buckeyes, and hemlocks reign; and the understory, a subroof of elegant dogwoods, mountain maples, mountain hollies, and other small trees that can survive on filtered sun.

Bridging the gap between understory and overstory, a variety of vines dangle from treetops and intertwine to form woody webs. Wrist-thick summer grape and frost grape vines reach 100 feet to the ground and sport clusters of seedy fruit that are treasures to bird and bear. Dutchman's-pipe grows in twisted ropes as thick as a bushel basket. Its valentine-shaped leaves and purple, pipe-shaped flowers make it both strikingly beautiful and easy to identify. So heavy do the woody vines grow that they eventually rip limbs from their host trees or drag entire arbors to the ground, creating ravaged landscapes many acres in size. Though forlorn in appearance, these vinelands, like the one along Husky Gap Trail, are hot spots for wildlife viewing.

This black bear cub (Ursus americanus) *seems to be testing its claws. Black bear sightings are possible throughout the spring, summer, and fall along the trails of the Smokies. Once widespread throughout much of North America, bears now thrive in the park's heavily wooded areas.*

One of the early spring wildflowers, the trout lily (Erythronium umbilicatum) has a tiny lemon-yellow flower and showy stamens. Its name comes from its mottled green and brown leaves, which are similar to the markings on a brook trout.

An old-growth forest is constantly in flux. When a 150-foot-tall tulip tree is toppled by winds or snow load, its absence creates a hole in the upper canopy that allows a flood of invigorating sunlight. Seeds and seedlings, languishing in the shade, receive the catalyst they have patiently waited for. Opportunists like Eastern hemlock, tulip tree, and Fraser magnolia now have their chance.

Such a giant does not fall quietly, however. As its bole crashes to the ground, its roots are torn from the rocky soil, leaving their own vacancy--a crater as large as a cement truck. The now vertical root system may stand 20 feet tall. As this action is repeated tens of thousands of times, the old-growth landscape becomes a rumpled carpet of pits and mounds. The craters are freshly ploughed soil where disturbance-dependent plants like blackberry and catchfly can get a start.

Even the fallen bole is an opportunity. Thick mats of sphagnum moss quickly colonize the trunk, followed by red spruce and yellow birch seedlings. Birches are especially adept at using logs as nurseries. Seedlings send their roots down the sides of the log and into the earth. After the log decays in 30 to 40 years, the birch, stranded on prop roots, resembles a bow-legged cowboy.

Just as Alaska's Matanuska Valley is famous for producing giant vegetables, the Great Smoky Mountains are mother to super-sized trees. Many species like mountain laurel, rosebay rhododendron, mountain holly, and alternate-leaved dogwood, which are considered shrubs elsewhere, achieve tree status in the Smokies. Thanks to plentiful rainfall spread evenly across the seasons, relatively mild winters, and protection as a national park, rhododendrons attain girths of two feet in circumference and stand better than 20 feet tall. According to American Forests' National Register of Big Trees, 13 species of native trees reach their greatest size (measured by height, circumference, and crown) in Great Smoky Mountains National Park. This is a higher tally than in any other national park or national forest land in the country, even though many of these preserves are several times the size of the Smokies.

The park's record trees include chestnut oak, red maple, Eastern hemlock, yellow buckeye, black cherry, red hickory, silver bell, Fraser magnolia, Allegheny serviceberry, striped maple, red spruce, devil's walkingstick, and cinnamon clethra. The largest of these leviathans is the 141-foot-tall, 23-foot-circumference red maple that grows in the Albright Grove area of the park. Larger trees do inhabit the Smokies, including 200-foot-tall white pines and 25-foot-circumference tulip trees, but they are shy of national champion status.

Other than light gaps created by windthrow trees, few natural openings exist in the dense forests of the Smokies. However, those that do are interesting places indeed. Grassy balds are meadows that dot the highlands of the southern Appalachian Mountains from Virginia down to North Georgia. Their moniker is derived from the fact that, compared to tree-covered lands, they are bald. Though the Cherokee referred to them hundreds of years ago, and early 18th-century surveyors documented their existence, the origin of the oldest grassy balds continues to puzzle ecologists. Theories include ice storms, grazing by buffalo and elk, burning by Native Americans, and combinations thereof.

Grassy balds are magnets for hikers because of the rare views they offer. Yet for botanists, these treeless zones offer even more. Atop Gregory and Andrews balds flourish naturally occurring flame azalea shrubs that challenge the beauty of any domestic garden in the world. In late June and early July they bloom in colors that range from white to peach to yellow to furnace red. Early botanists were so impressed that they took cuttings from the azaleas on Gregory Bald and added them to the collection at the British Museum of Natural History.

Other notable plants also populate the balds, including purple-flowered Catawba rhododendron, blueberry bushes ten feet tall, and mountain oat grass. The latter species, because it abhors shade, is found in few other places in the park beyond the balds.

From the 1800s until park establishment in 1934, farmers used the grassy balds to graze livestock. Each year, thousands of sheep, cows, pigs, and horses were herded to the high country and pastured there from spring through fall. The farmers cut and burned to enlarge existing balds and to create new ones from forested ridgetops. Since the park service took over the land and curtailed grazing, trees have begun reclaiming the balds--curiously, even the balds that existed prior to settlement by Europeans. Rangers now must periodically mow and trim the balds to fend off the encroaching forest.

The lofty Eastern hemlocks at Albright Grove are pieces of one of the park's most impressive old-growth forests. The Eastern hemlock (Tsuga canadensis) *is a pyramid-shaped evergreen with heavy foliage and upsweeping branches. Albright Grove was named for National Park Service co-founder Horace Albright.*

The yellow poplar or tulip tree (Liriodendron tulipfera) *flanked by ferns on the Ramsey Cascades Trail is a member of the magnolia family. Tulip trees can grow to five feet in diameter.*

In the southern Appalachians, individual flowering dogwoods (Cornus florida) *may grow up to forty feet tall. More modest examples are also frequently found in the forest understory. Songbirds, including the American Robin, are attracted to the fruit of the flowering dogwood.*

This showy Catawba rhododendron offers large clusters of flowers that range from pink to deep purple in early summer. It grows in dense thickets on mountain summits and cliff edges in the Smokies.

A footpath wanders between a yellow birch tree (Betula alleghaniensis) *and Catawba rhododendron.*

One of the most magnificent Appalachian mountain shrubs, the flame azalea (Rhododendron calendulaceum) produces larger flowers than most native shrubs. The loose clusters may be orange, yellow, or red.

A member of the impatiens family, the spotted touch-me-not (Impatiens capensis), or jewelweed, is very attractive to hummingbirds.

The fire pink (Silene virginica) is actually red. A member of the carnation family, it is also known as the catchfly for its sticky stems and calyx that sometimes trap insects.

Early saxifrage (Saxifragia virginensis) *grows beside streams and in other moist areas.*

Cow parsnips (Heracleum maximum) *growing on a hillside push their blossoms above a carpet of white snakeroot* (Ageratina altissima). *The scientific name for the cow parsnip refers to Hercules, who is said to have used it for medicine. White snakeroot was used by Indians to treat poisonous snakebites and other ailments.*

What appear to be large, white petals of the flowering dogwood are in fact modified leaves or "bracts." The tiny yellowish-green cluster in the center are the real flowers.

A small tree or large shrub, the eastern redbud (Cercis canadensis) flowers in the spring before other trees form leaves. Its magenta flowers appear all over the tree and sometimes seem to have sprung from the bark.

Foxtail grass (Seteria faberi) is a non-native or exotic grass introduced into the Smoky Mountains. Several states consider it an invasive weed.

Fragrant white azaleas are among the last flowers to bloom in the spring. White azaleas have inspired at least one folk song: "When the White Azaleas Start Blooming."

Squirrel corn (Dicentra canadensis) is a spring plant found in wooded areas of the park. Its fragrant white flowers are purple tinged, and its tubers look like grains of corn.

One of the most plentiful trees in the Smokies, the tulip tree has large four-lobed leaves and greenish-yellow tulip-shaped flowers with orange markings. The tallest of American hardwoods, the tulip tree sometimes grows in large stands.

The Franklinia tree (Franklinia alatamaha), with its large, white, camellia-like flowers, is named after Benjamin Franklin. Believed to be extinct in the wild and not native to the Smokies, existing trees descend from those propagated by the botanists John and William Bartram, who discovered it in 1765.

The yellow-fringed orchid (Platanthera ciliaris) is a showy orange perennial. With fringe-lipped flowers, the orchid blooms throughout the summer. It can reach a height of twenty-four inches.

A poisonous mushroom, fly amanita mushroom (Amanita muscaria) is one of well over 2,000 species of fungi in the Smoky Mountains. Yellow or red with white spots, it often grows in the shadow of hardwood trees or conifers.

Wild columbine (Aquilegia canadensis) *blooms in the spring and early summer in rocky woodlands and along the banks of streams. Like other red wildflowers, the columbine attracts hummingbirds. Its graceful flowers, which resemble small cornucopias, have inspired poets.*

This sourwood tree (Oxydendrum arboreum) *in the Cataloochee Valley wears bright fall colors. Mature sourwood trees have a natural crook in their trunks; settlers used this wood for sled runners. The Cataloochee Valley supported the largest settlement in the Smokies in the late 19th century. Cataloochee, the Cherokee word for "standing tall," refers to the tall spruce and fir trees on the mountains flanking the valley.*

A colorful final act before the arrival of cold weather, asters bloom prolifically in the late summer and early fall along with white snakeroot. Native aster varieties grow wild in a wide range of environments. White snakeroot can reach a height of six feet.

A Mountain Laurel (Kalmia latifolia) *framed by a fog-shrouded tree.*

Known variously as Virginia meadow beauties or "handsome Harry," Rhexia virginica *has tiny purplish flowers surrounding a yellow pistil and stamens.*

Showy orchis (Galearis spectabilis *or* Orchis spectabilis) *is also known as the purple-hooded orchid. This woodland plant boasts striking flowers of violet and white and is one of the earliest orchids to bloom in the spring.*

Rosebay rhododendron (Rhododendron maximum) *is known as "great laurel." The shrub produces rose to white flowers in June and July. Rosebay rhododendrons are an important part of the park's evergreen understory.*

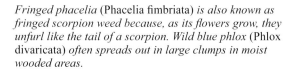

Fringed phacelia (Phacelia fimbriata) *is also known as fringed scorpion weed because, as its flowers grow, they unfurl like the tail of a scorpion. Wild blue phlox* (Phlox divaricata) *often spreads out in large clumps in moist wooded areas.*

WONDERLAND

The ubiquitous black-eyed Susan (Rudbeckia hirta) *appeals to a great variety of butterflies. This flower has attracted an orange sulphur* (Colias eurytheme). *Prevalent throughout most of the U.S., the orange sulphur is also known as the alfalfa butterfly since its caterpillars feed on legumes like alfalfa and clover.*

A walk along a winding, tree-shaded path in the Great Smoky Mountains is a sensuous delight. Brilliant green and yellow warblers chip, twitter, and sing as they fly from branch to branch. Sparkling streams giggle over ancient boulders and water-worn stones. In a sunny spot, pine needle duff and galax exhale their tangy smells, while higher, in a shady cove, trillium and lichen scent the air. Objects both animate and still beckon to be touched: the furrowed bark of an ash tree, a deep, spongy bed of moss, the shell of a box turtle.

Every alert visitor to the Great Smoky Mountains is, in a very real sense, an explorer. So rich and varied are the park's ecological zones that scientists estimate, conservatively, that 100,000 different types of plants and animals live here. Only about 13,000 have been identified so far. In the 1980s, a hiker discovered a large grove of paper birch trees, a presence that had gone undetected despite centuries of human habitation. Rangers leading groups of tourists along well-worn trails have sighted butterflies and wildflowers previously unknown in the region. Junior high and high school students volunteering for the park have collected hundreds of moths, some species not only new to the Smokies, but new to the science books.

Turning over a trailside rock may reveal one of the park's 30 or so species of salamanders. If you are quick, you may even contain one of the wriggling amphibians in the cupped palm of your hand. These benign, often colorful creatures are some of the hidden treasures of the Great Smoky Mountains. Biologists proclaim the Smokies "The Salamander Capital of the World" with more different types of salamanders than any similar-sized area on Earth. Even after a century of research, a new species is discovered in the park every few years. One, the red-cheeked salamander, is an endemic; it lives only within the boundaries of the national park. If you turn off the Blue Ridge Parkway in the vicinity of Balsam Mountain Campground, and drive along Heintooga Ridge Road, you will, within the span of only three or four miles, pass from the realm of the southern gray-cheeked salamander to that of the red-cheeked salamander, two closely related species that, nonetheless, occupy distinct, barely overlapping ranges.

Indeed, if engineers were to design a mountain range to efficiently maximize the variety of flora and fauna within the constraints of limited space and material, that mountain range might logically be placed in the southeastern United States and resemble the Great Smokies.

The highest peaks of the Smokies are cloaked with a dense growth of red spruce and Fraser fir trees, an evergreen zone not unlike the great boreal forest that stretches from the northeastern United States far into Canada. Yet a pair of hikers picking their way along the rocky tread of the Appalachian Trail, enveloped by spruce and fir, can look down to, say, Wear Valley, eight miles distant and 4,000 feet lower, and see a southern pine-oak forest typical of South Carolina or North Georgia—a dry woods where chameleon-like green anoles bask in the summer's heat and mockingbirds call incessantly from persimmon trees.

That North and South co-exist so near to one another makes for many interesting contrasts and comminglings. For instance, juncos are bold little birds that spend their winters in the foothills and valleys of the Smoky Mountains. Come spring, one

*In its juvenile stage, the red spotted newt (*Notophthalmus viridescens) *is called the red eft. Its bright color warns possible predators of its poisonous skin. Adult newts are olive green with a yellow underside.*

The fishing spider (Dolomedes triton) *sits on top of water and waits for prey such as insect larvae and small fish. It also dives under water, where it can remain submerged for long periods.*

subspecies of junco migrates north hundreds of miles to find suitable breeding grounds in the northern forests; another group simply flies upslope to the Smoky Mountain high country, where they also find good boreal homes.

The black-capped chickadee ranges as far north as central Alaska and reaches the southern edge of its territory in the highlands of the Smokies. Its southern cousin, the Carolina chickadee, lives throughout the Deep South and lower Midwest and finds amenable habitat in the valleys of the Smokies. The southern Appalachian Mountains are one of the few areas where the ranges of the two species meet.

Altitude, however, is only one of the structural aspects of the Great Smoky Mountains that nurture biological diversity. The Smokies are a chaotic jumble of folds, ridges, valleys, and bulges, a notable contrast to the typically neat rows of ridges and valleys in the Rocky Mountains. A south-facing slope looming above Cades Cove bakes in the afternoon sun and absorbs the same amount of heat as flat ground 1,300 miles to the south. The north side of the same mountain, almost perpetually shaded by itself and other, higher peaks, will still hold snow a week after it has melted from the south, west, and east aspects.

The vegetation on the southern exposure is dominated by drought-tolerant evergreen trees with specially modified leaves to slow water loss (pines), and shrubs and forbs with thick, waxy leaves (mountain laurel, blueberry, galax, and trailing arbutus). The forest floor is a deep, acidic, rust-colored mat of pine needles. Scaly, fast-moving lizards called skinks stalk flies on sun-warmed tree trunks. Meanwhile, at the same elevation on the north side,

basswoods, tulip trees, maples, silver bell, hemlock, and flowering dogwood prosper in rich, moist soils. On the forest floor, a crazy quilt of wildflowers bloom each spring: trilliums, Dutchman's breeches, hepatica, anemone, trout lily, bishop's cap, and wild oats. Woodland salamanders, which must keep their skin moist to breathe, rest in the cool dark pockets beneath logs and stones.

Even the shape of a mountain affects the life it hosts. Bowl-shaped Appalachian coves collect soils eroded from the slopes above, and they hold moisture as well, two reasons why most of the park's champion trees are found in sheltered coves. Conversely, out on the nose of a ridge, water is shunted away, leaving the rocky soils much drier.

Though an omnivorous black bear may lumber to the rain-soaked high country in summer to feast on berries and return to the sunny lowlands in fall for oak acorns, many other inhabitants of the Great Smoky Mountains are less mobile and more specialized. For these plants and animals, the structure of the mountains, combined with long-term changes in climate, have had a fascinating effect on biological diversity.

When the Pleistocene Epoch began 1.6 million years ago, the basic form of the Great Smoky Mountains was much as it is today. But frequent changes in climate, flip-flopping between ice age and inter-glacier warm-up (when average temperatures were sometimes warmer than today's) caused a perpetual yo-yoing of Appalachian flora and fauna. As mile-thick glaciers advanced into the Great Lakes region and northern Ohio, northern species were gradually dislocated from mountain to valley, some retreating as far as the Atlantic coastal plain or Mexico.

Yet one species' loss is another's gain. For example, the cold-tolerant *Boreus brumalis,* or snow scorpionfly, which was forced south by the approaching glaciers, discovered a perfectly comfortable new home high in the ice age Smokies. During the most severe of the 20 or so Pleistocene cold spells, permanent snow fields lingered on Mt. Le Conte and Clingmans Dome and on the north slopes of other high peaks. *Boreus,* which unlike most insects, can remain active at temperatures around 32° F., and is often seen crawling across the snow, thrived a mile high in the Smokies just as it had in inter-glacier Canada.

A few tens of thousands of years later, when the climate changed again and the Tropics advanced northward and the Arctic retreated, many Smoky mountain insects were Canada bound and many Deep South bugs were Smokies bound.

But again, interesting things happen in mountains. As the Pleistocene dragged on, *Boreus* and some of its relatives adapted to climate changes by simply moving downhill during cold periods and up during warm. Throughout the 10,000-year-long warm-up we are currently experiencing, a population of Boreus has been stranded above elevations of 4,000 feet in the Smokies. Elsewhere in North America, Boreus can be found only in places once covered by glaciers. No doubt this southern, disjunct population of scorpion flies is beginning to differ in subtle ways from the main population hundreds of miles to the north.

Such was the case with a group of little brown beetles of the genus *Trechus.* Like *Boreus,* a single species of *Trechus* was stranded along the State Line Ridge (which the Appalachian Trail traverses) of the Smokies when the climate warmed. Because lowlands, with different flora and fauna, separate this ridge from others, *Trechus* was deterred from moving to adjacent territories. As the climate warmed even more, low gaps in the ridge, where weather, flora, and fauna differed subtly, began to separate the original population into several subsets. Over thousands of generations, the isolated populations began to differ from one another, until today, when scientists recognize at least a dozen distinct species of *Trechus* spaced along the knobs of the Smokies' highest ridges.

Most black bears (Ursus americanus) *in Great Smoky Mountains National Park weigh between 100 and 300 pounds. Scientists estimate that about 1,500 bears live in the park.*

Known for its hinged shell, which allows almost complete retraction to avoid danger, the eastern box turtle (Terrapene carolina) *is common in Great Smoky Mountains National Park. Markings on the brown carapace vary widely in color and pattern.*

The Red-cheeked salamander (Plethodon jordani) *is found only within Great Smoky Mountains National Park. It is one of thirty species in the park, which has the most varied salamander fauna in the United States.*

Unregulated hunting, roaming packs of dogs, and unsound logging practices caused white-tailed deer to nearly disappear from the Great Smoky Mountains. Protection as a national park has allowed the population to recover.

The northern copperhead (Agkistrodon contortrix) *is one of two species of poisonous snakes in the Smokies; the other is the timber rattlesnake. The adult copperhead is carnivorous and consumes mice, small birds, lizards, and insects.*

The northern walkingstick (Diapheromera femorata) *has many names, from "prairie alligator" to "devil's horse." It eats the leaves of oak, basswood, and wild cherry trees. With its stick-like body and long legs resembling twigs, it can easily blend in with the trees on which it lives.*

The northern fence lizard (Sceloporus undulates) *is a species of horned lizard. This prolific climber resides in pine-oak forests.*

Cope's gray treefrog (Hyla chrysoscelis) *is found near bodies of water in forest environments. This greenish-gray frog makes a trilled or pulsed call during breeding season.*

These four red fox (Vulpes vulpes) *kits are exploring just outside their den entrance. Solitary in nature, the red fox is a skilled hunter. Its den is usually located to provide a commanding view of its surroundings. This reddish fox has white underparts, chin, and throat; a white-tipped tail; and black feet and lower legs.*

A young raccoon surveys the forest from its den in a hollow sycamore tree. Both the raccoon (Procyon lotor) *and the sycamore* (Platanus occidentalis) *reside streamside in the Smokies. Sycamores frequently grow to massive sizes; their mottled brown, white, and green "camouflage" bark sloughs off easily.*

One of two "punctuation" anglewing butterflies, the question mark butterfly (Polygonia interrogationis) has a pearlish comma-like marking and dot on the underside of its hindwings that appears to form a question mark. With its orange and dark brown or black blotches, it is very difficult to see when resting on tree bark.

Though the appearance of the coral hairstreak (Harkenclenus titus) may vary, it is distinguished by a row of bright coral spots along the edge of its hind wings. Butterflies are attracted to the brilliant orange flowers of butterfly weed (Asclepias variegata).

The insect-eating praying mantis, with its forelegs raised in prayer-like fashion, disguises itself as part of the plant on which it rests. The mantis pictured here is praying on a species of teasel, an exotic biennial or short-lived perennial that competes for space with native plants.

Though they vary considerably in appearance, the checkered skipper (Pyrgus communis) *tends to be brownish gray with white checkering. They fly in a quick darting manner that makes them appear to "skip" over plants.*

The eastern tailed blue butterfly (Everes comyntas) *is small and described as flying on "gossamer wings." Its lower wings are silver gray with black dots. Orange patches mark the outside of each hind wing. The color of the upper wing varies between the sexes.*

Polyphemus (Antherea polyphemus) *is a large silk moth known for its hind-wing eyespots. Named for the legendary one-eyed giant Polyphemus, the eyespots help protect it from predators by attracting attackers away from the moth's head.*

The common buckeye butterfly (Junonia coenia *or* Precis lavinia coenia) *is brown with orange markings and prominent eyespots. Its habitat includes meadows, roadsides, the edges of swamps, and other open spots.*

One of the earth's most ancient living creatures, this aquatic dragonfly (Odonata) *can be seen hovering and darting in search of insect prey near fresh water. There are more than 450 dragonfly species in North America alone, with colorful names ranging from "devil's darning needle" to "water witch."*

The bobcat (Felis rufus), *a secretive, nocturnal mammal, usually weighs between ten and thirty-five pounds. An expert hunter, it feeds on small mammals and birds.*

Expert climbers when they are awake, black bears sleep either in trees or on the ground. Indians and Appalachian farmers hunted the bear for meat, clothing, income, and sport.

This eastern screech owl (Otus asio) *roosts during the day in a large sycamore tree. Reddish screech owls are more common in the southern states, while gray ones predominate in the north. Instead of building their own nests, these owls live in hollow tree stumps or nests made by other birds. Their call is actually a trill or a descending whinny, rather than a screech.*

The northern bobwhite (Colinus virginianus) *is found infrequently in Great Smoky Mountains National Park, although it may be spotted in places like Cades Cove or other open areas. Although the bobwhite's range extends through the eastern U.S., its population is declining.*

Year-round occupants of the Smokies, red-tailed hawks (Buteo jamaicensis) *are very territorial. Their diet varies with the season, although rabbits and rodents are preferred fare.*

The bright red plumage of the adult male cardinal (Cardinalis cardinalis) *provides a striking color contrast in a wintry setting. Male and female cardinals have vibrant singing voices, and counter-singing is an important part of their courtship ritual.*

Though pictured here among crab apple blossoms, the cedar waxwing (Bombycilla cedrorum) *takes its name from the cedar berries, of which it is so fond, as well as the waxy red tips on its wing feathers. The cedar waxwing's black mask, crest, and yellow-brown plumage make it easy to identify. These gregarious birds are generally found in open areas. Most of the adult bird's diet consists of berries, flowers, and tree sap.*

A female ruby-throated hummingbird (Archilochus colubris) *feeds here on a trumpet creeper* (Campsis radicans), *a high-climbing semi-woody vine. The only hummingbird species native to the eastern U.S., the ruby-throated hummingbird feeds on the nectar of more than thirty plants, but prefers the nectar from tubular, red flowers like those of the trumpet creeper.*

A year-round resident in Great Smoky Mountains National Park, the American goldfinch (Carduelis tristis) *prefers habitats such as overgrown fields, roadsides, orchards and gardens. It is the state bird of Iowa, New Jersey, and Washington.*

"Dendroica" means tree dweller, and this yellow-throated warbler (Dendroica dominica) *nests in the tree canopy, preferring pine, sycamore, and, in warm places, cypress swamps and oaks draped with Spanish moss.*

The great horned owl (Bubo virginianus) *is the largest owl in the southern U.S. Its name acknowledges the owl's ear tufts resembling horns. This solitary bird of prey inhabits dense woodlands and does most of its hunting at night.*

Strutting and gobbling, this large wild turkey (Meleagris gallopavo) *performs a courtship ritual. Its habitat includes open woodlands and mature forests, where it forages for a diet that includes seeds and acorns, insects, and salamanders.*

The indigo bunting (Passerina cyanea) *is a familiar songbird quite common in Great Smoky Mountains National Park. The iridescent blue plumage that the male displays during breeding season is not pigment-based but instead depends on the diffraction of light through its feathers.*

With his black-and-white coloring and rose-red breast patch, the rose-breasted grosbeak (Pheucticus ludovicianus) *is easy to recognize. The grosbeak's song is similar to the American Robin's but is more melodious.*

FALLING WATER

Rushing mountain streams and waterfalls enhance the wilderness experience as they cascade through the forest here. There are 400 streams and 150 headwaters within the parkway's boundaries.

When slow moving low-pressure systems drift into the Southeast, local meteorologists declare "the tap is wide open," and band after band of super-humid Gulf of Mexico air flows northward. As this air is forced upward by the southern Appalachian Mountains, it cools beyond its ability to hold so much moisture. Rain falls for hours or days, and pretty mountain streams turn to great frothing torrents that spill from their banks. If you stand beside a stream at such times you can hear, above the pounding of rain on your poncho, the growl of rocks rolling downstream. When the clouds finally clear, streamers of mist curl upward like smoke, and distant mountains shine like polished stones.

Precipitation has nowhere to pause or languish in the Smokies. Because there were no glaciers so far south, there are no scoured places for natural ponds or lakes. Consequently, aside from the man-made lakes on the park's boundaries, standing water is almost nonexistent.

Along the highest ridges, rain is either absorbed by roots, drawn into the rocky ground, or routed downhill along the surface. Most of the rain that goes underground is diverted to the surface a short way downslope, where it trickles from the ground as springs. Owing partly to geology and partly to climate, the Smokies have an unusual number of springs and small streams near their summits. There is a famous spring near Le Conte Lodge, just below the top of Mt. Le Conte, which has been a reliable water source for years. Travelers on the Appalachian Trail depend on springs that seep from just below the ridgetops. Along trails like Road Prong and Low Gap, hikers follow small mountain streams nearly to the spine of the mountain range.

On down the mountain, springs played a role in the 19th-century pioneer history of the area. Settlers searched their properties for a reliable spring with a good "bold" flow before deciding where to build their homes. Some mountaineers grew so fond of the taste of the water that burbled from their old farmstead spring that they returned years after the establishment of the national park to fill jugs with drinking water.

Springs feed the more than 1,000 miles of streams and rivers that rush through the national park today. Except for short periods following a deluge (or "gully-washer" in the local parlance), these waterways flow absolutely clear. Most of the larger streams are boulder-strewn with massive chunks of sandstone that broke from tall cliffs, probably during the Pleistocene, and migrated down steep slopes into the valley bottoms. Water, and the minute grit it carries, has worn the older rocks as smooth as bowling balls. In streams with a relatively stable flow, the tops of these boulders are covered with thick moss and even wildflowers; but boulders (called "graybacks") in flood-prone drainages are always bare.

At least 50 kinds of fish inhabit park waters, from minnow-class species like shiners, dace, chubs, madtoms, stonerollers, and sculpins to a variety of game fish that include rock bass, smallmouth bass, rainbow trout, brook trout, and brown trout. Most of their diets are made up of small aquatic insects, including caddis flies and mayflies, along with terrestrials like ants, spiders, crickets, and inch worms that stray too close to the water.

Brook trout are the only trout native to the southern Appalachian Mountains. A cold-water species, they

In spring and summer, thick foliage hides part of Tom Branch Falls. This seventy-five-foot waterfall begins as a single trickle and becomes three fifteen-foot-high trickles, then two sixteen-foot streams, before ending in numerous streamlets coursing over a ledge into Deep Creek.

Cataloochee Creek, pictured here in early autumn, is the main stream flowing through this remote southeastern section of Great Smoky Mountains National Park. The creek is a popular trout fishing spot.

are near the southern limit of their range in the Great Smokies. The logging boom, which lasted from the late 1890s through 1939, took a heavy toll on brook trout. As steep mountainsides were clear-cut and burned, soil eroded into the streams, choking the native trout and burying their spawning beds. Cutting trees from the banks increased sunlight on streams and riversides, causing water temperatures to rise. Temperature-sensitive brookies responded by moving into the cooler headwaters. Building and dynamiting temporary splash dams and running rafts of logs down the larger streams also harmed fisheries.

Introducing non-native rainbow trout to park streams made life even harder for brookies. Rainbows grow larger than brook trout and are therefore valued more highly by many anglers. However, these larger, more aggressive newcomers have kept the natives out of their preferred habitat in mid- and lower-elevation rivers and confined them to marginal streams at the higher elevations.

One feature of Smoky Mountain streams that has spared brook trout an even gloomier fate is the waterfall. Most rainbows were stocked at the more accessible, lower elevation streams. Waterfalls prevented them from moving far enough upstream to completely displace the brook trout. Today waterfalls often mark the boundary between brook trout waters and rainbow trout habitats.

Waterfalls are, of course, important to people as well. The trails to Grotto, Laurel, and Rainbow falls are some of the most heavily used in the park. Height-wise, Smoky Mountain waterfalls are midgets compared to those in other national parks like Yosemite and Yellowstone or even nearby Nantahala

National Forest. The Smokies' tallest, Ramsey Cascades, is a mere 100 feet of stair step ledges.

But what Smoky Mountain waterfalls lack in stature, they make up for in lush, wild beauty. Laurel Falls is so-named because it is framed by hundreds of pink mountain laurel blossoms in May. Even when not in bloom, the evergreen mountain laurel leaves lend depth and contrast to the sparkling water of the falls.

In June, when the Catawba rhododendron surrounding Ramsey Cascades is heavy with purple blooms, painters and photographers make the four-mile pilgrimage to the site to attempt to capture the scene. Half the splendor of Grotto Falls is the dark jungle of vegetation that surrounds it.

The potential of falling water did not go unnoticed by early human inhabitants. The Cherokee built water-powered pounding mills to crush their corn. Pounding mills are giant mortars and pestles in which the pestle is raised as water fills a vessel at one end and falls when the vessel tips and empties.

Baskins Falls, near present day Gatlinburg, is said to have served as a warm weather shower for families that lived in the area. The same families built small but complex tub mills beside the faster flowing streams. The racing waters turned a handmade wooden turbine that delivered power to the heavy round millstone that turned and ground the corn. Not everyone chose to expend the time and resources necessary to have their own mill, but doing so saved them the 10 to 12 percent toll at the big custom mills.

At Mingus Mill, near Oconaluftee, the water-powered turbine ran two sets of millstones and an ingenious vertical conveyor belt that transported wheat flour to the second floor. There it was separated into different grades, ranging from mostly bran for animal feed to special white flour for cakes and other pastries.

Cable Mill, which still stands beside Mill Creek in Cades Cove, once cut timber and ground corn. Its water-powered sash saw made some 50 strokes per minute and cut some of the lumber that can still be seen in houses that the park service has preserved in the cove.

At ninety feet, Laurel Falls is one of the highest waterfalls in the Smokies. The upper section of the fall is pictured here. Its lower section cascades nearly fifty feet into a pool.

During the 19th century, flocks of passenger pigeons frequented the Smokies and Little Pigeon River is named after them.

Trillium, from the Latin word for three, is an apt name for a plant with three leaves, three petals, and a flower with three sepals. This wake robin (Trillium erectum) is one of nine different members of the species found in Great Smoky Mountains National Park.

Many streams in the Smokies boast a waterfall. Indian Creek features two thick parallel streams of water in a twenty-five-foot cascade.

Autumn view of Indian Creek Falls. Located in the Deep Creek area, Indian Creek Falls may be reached via a two-mile roundtrip hike from a nearby campground. No place in the Southeast attracts more leaf-watchers than the Smokies, and this autumn view suggest why that is so.

Scenic Rainbow Falls creates a fine spray as it drops water eighty feet over ledges. A rainbow is often visible on sunny days. During the winter a cone of ice may form at the base of the falls.

A winter snow fall transforms the woods around Cosby Creek as it flows through the northeastern corner of Great Smoky Mountains National Park. This area was once known as the "moonshine capital of the world."

Located in the north central section of Great Smoky Mountains National Park, Grotto Falls is the only waterfall in the park that visitors can walk behind without getting soaked.

The Little River becomes larger as it progresses through Great Smoky Mountains National Park. Here it pours over a waterfall at the Sinks.

A walk along Trillium Gap Trail, through a hemlock-dominated forest, leads to Grotto Falls, a waterfall of twenty-five feet shown here amidst fall color.

At twenty feet high, Abrams Falls is one of the most picturesque waterfalls in Great Smoky Mountains National Park. It is named after Old Abram, the Cherokee chief of Chilhowee, a village once located near the mouth of Abrams Creek.

Laden with boulders, Big Creek flows beneath a luxuriant forest canopy. With its natural resources protected from development, Great Smoky Mountains National Park was named an International Biosphere Reserve in 1976.

After a heavy rain, water in Le Conte Creek sluices through the streambed sweeping over everything in its path. On average, more than 85 inches of rain fall annually in some parts of the Smokies, contributing significantly to the streams that flow through Great Smoky Mountains National Park.

Cascading through the forest, Le Conte Creek flows from Great Smoky Mountains National Park to Gatlinburg, Tennessee. It was formerly known as Mill Creek, for the many gristmills that it powered.

Located in the Qualla Boundary near Cherokee, North Carolina, Mingo Falls is a dramatic 120-foot-high cascade. A central ledge divides water in the falls, sending some along a single narrow stream on the left, while water flows through numerous rivulets and cascades on the right

Mountain Laurel (Kalmia latifolia) *blooms along the West Prong of the Little Pigeon River. Each mountain laurel blossom looks like a tiny, open umbrella. Early mountain settlers called this plant "ivy" and reserved the name "mountain laurel" for the larger-leafed rhododendron.*

Daylilies (Hemerocallis) *bloom along the Little Pigeon River. This spreading perennial derives its scientific name from the Greek words for "beauty" and "day," appropriate for a flower that lasts just one day. With its multiple buds, an entire clump of daylilies can flower for several weeks.*

In the Smokies autumn is the driest time of the year, with warm days and cool nights. Late September brings the first frosts. The season also offers dramatic settings like this one around Little River.

The Oconaluftee River begins in the high country of Great Smoky Mountains National Park and flows southwest through Cherokee, North Carolina, before it meets the Tuckasegee River.

By the early 1800s, Euro-American settlers had established homesteads along the banks of the Oconaluftee River.

At 100 feet, Ramsey Cascades is the highest waterfall that can be reached from a trail in Great Smoky Mountains National Park. Water flows over a sandstone bluff before crashing against boulders at the base of the falls.

Clear and cool, Big Creek is a popular hiking and fishing area. The forty-five-foot-high Mouse Creek Falls occur where two streams of water flow over a high ledge and then meet in a rock hollow, with the biggest stream then splitting into four separate falls.

HOMELAND

Secluded Hyatt Lane crosses the rich meadows and forests of Cades Cove. The scenic lane makes a nice shortcut across the loop road for persons short on time.

On one of your visits to the Great Smoky Mountains, take time to visit the remains of a true hardscrabble mountain farmstead. Not the deep-soiled, prosperous valley farms in Cades Cove or Cataloochee, but the rocky, steep-sloped, seat-of-your-pants, do or die farms in places like Roaring Fork or Bradley Fork or the upper Sugarlands.

You will find a chimney, only half still standing, and perhaps a shallow depression that describes the shape of the 16- by 20-foot log home. There will be a spring or stream nearby, or both. The spring will be trickling from a hillside, and by looking closely, you can discern how the head of the spring was dug out and artfully lined with stones to create a pleasant place to fill a bucket. The landscaping may have survived the house. A black walnut tree was planted for its shade and delicious nuts, red cedar for the chickens to roost, and boxwood, daffodils, and hyacinth because they were pretty.

A stand of nearly identical, arrow-straight tulip trees, now 80 feet tall, marks the site of the old cornfield. Conspicuous piles of rock, most watermelon-sized or larger, usually stacked upon one large, immovable boulder, document countless days of field cleaning labor.

Now imagine it is 1840, that you are on horseback, and that you have come to start a new life on this unsettled land. Make it April. The mountainside is covered with virgin forest. Flowering dogwood and sprawling beds of phacelia and trout lilies are blooming. Tiny buds are unfurling on the great maple trees like brilliant green ornaments.

You have some Scots-Irish in your past. At least one of your grandparents crossed the Atlantic during the "great migration" (1717-1776), driven by drought, poverty, or religious persecution courtesy of the English. Your ancestors' home may have been in Northern Ireland, perhaps County Antrim, Down, Londonderry, or Tyrone; or they may have come from County Donegal in the Republic of Ireland.

As a group, your forefathers were characterized as brave, uncompromising, independent, and occasionally belligerent. Whether from paintings or stories or just plain instinct, the green slopes of the southern Appalachians look a bit like home.

Certainly you must feel some apprehension, a sense of loss for those left behind in Virginia or piedmont North Carolina, and anxieties about surviving on this rough land. But would you not feel exhilaration, too? A flood of inspirations and possibilities? Are you likely to ever experience similar emotions so pure and strong today?

The wonder we feel when exploring old homesites has a lot to do with the enormous gulf in lifestyles between yesterday and today. Basic human nature has probably changed little in the last 4,000 years, but in the last 150 years alone, the changes in how we spend the hours of our days have been astonishing.

Mid-19th-century mountain families did not shop for a new home on the internet; they built it with their own hands and own basic hand tools. Most men could build a fireplace and chimney, split shingles for a roof, hew planks for a floor, frame a steeply pitched roof, make a chair from maple and corn shucks, and construct a workable land sled. With the help of a few neighbors, the mountain man could transform a half dozen chestnut trees or tulip trees into a barn, home, church, or school--some of which would remain

The Elijah Oliver house in Cades Cove is surrounded by out-buildings that help depict the life of the area's farm families. A barn below the cabin, a smokehouse next to the kitchen, a springhouse, and a corncrib are located nearby.

The Mountain Farm Museum hosts two annual events: "Women's Work," in June, which honors the varied roles of rural women of the past, and the "Mountain Life Festival," in September, which demonstrates traditional fall activities, including molasses-making.

Though many structures were moved from their original sites, the mill, millrace, and dam are in their original locations at Cades Cove. A water-powered gristmill of this size could grind more than 100 pounds of corn in an hour, far more than a family's tub mill could produce.

standing well into the 21st century. Chances are he could repair a harness, make a door hinge, fix a plow, build a coffin, repair shoes, and maybe even make a rifle stock and barrel.

The typical mountain woman had the skills to transform both wool and flax into cloth and cloth into clothes. She could take worn-out dresses, old sacks, and cotton from the garden and make a warm, beautiful quilt that would be sought after by affluent collectors a century later. She could sulfur apples and make a pie from flour, lard, salt, honey, and berries picked that morning. She knew how to help another woman bring a child into the world and how to treat 50 different ailments with nothing more than leaves, twigs, and roots from the woods.

Today's ready-to-serve meals are the antithesis of our mountaineer family's 1840 repast. Nearly all of the food the mountain family consumed came directly from their own efforts. To get the corn for their corn bread, the family first had to clear 10 acres of old-growth trees with an ax. Then came the rocks, and then dragging a plow through soil as tough as burlap. The corn had to be planted at the right time of year (when oak leaves were the size of squirrel ears), and good luck had to keep late frosts, hail, drought, blight, and early frosts at bay. Keeping raccoons, crows, deer, and bears at bay required more direct action and was part of the reason the family long rifle was hung above the front doorway. If all went favorably, come fall they would have several acres of 12-foot-tall Hickory King corn to harvest stalk by stalk, ear by ear, all by hand. Unfortunately the hard-won fruit of their efforts, the golden kernel of corn, was inedible unless it was cooked for hours in lye (to make hominy), or ground

into meal. Grinding entailed building a streamside tub mill with a tricky wooden turbine and matched round millstones, or hauling the corn to the closest community gristmill.

Even a simple food like green beans had to be painstakingly weeded throughout the summer and protected from all manner of pest and vermin, including insects, hogs, and children. Upon harvest, the beans needed to be either strung on thread and dried in the sun or pickled in a big crock and protected in the springhouse.

Certainly our modern lifestyle and that of the 19th-century mountain family differ in their relationship to the natural world. For the latter, weather was more than a topic of idle conversation. An extended summer dry spell could completely destroy a family's crops and garden, forcing them to abandon their land and move in with a more fortunate relative. A rainy week in December meant the whole family was confined to their cold, dark house with little in the way of amusement or diversion.

Yet nature brought boon more often than bust. Fresh, nutritious greens, such as pokeweed and ramps, awaited harvest in the forest each spring. Blackberries, blueberries, and huckleberries could be eaten as soon as they were picked or saved for jams and pies. Brook trout filled the rivers and streams. Walnuts and chestnuts rained from tall trees. A well-tended garden promised cabbage, potatoes, tomatoes, beans, squash, turnips, carrots, and hot peppers, each infinitely more flavorful than the pretty, yet bland, produce available in modern supermarkets. The limbs of orchard trees bowed each autumn from the weight of cherries, plums, peaches, and six varieties of apples.

Parents taught children the uses for over a hundred plants that grew wild in the woods: spicewood for tea and seasoning, touch-me-not to ease the itch of poison ivy, sweet gum for candy, galax and ground cedar for selling to the florist in Knoxville or Asheville, black locust trees for fence posts that never rot, white oak for shingles and baskets, dogwood for the shuttle of a loom, Fraser fir sap to sell for medicine, red cedar for keeping moths out of wool, and sourwood trunks for the curved runners of sleds.

The animals of the forest were not strangers, either. The poisonous snakes, northern copperheads and timber rattlesnakes, seemed to be always on people's minds. Men sometimes wore knee-high leather boots for protection, and children were taught to stay clear of rocky areas where venomous snakes were likely to be encountered. And it often fell upon the children to sweep the "yards" around the cabin down to bare dirt to discourage snakes from the vicinity.

The call of a yellow-billed cuckoo foretold rain; the sudden appearance of juncos meant snow was in the mountains. The nearness to the ground of a hornet's nest and the bands on woolly worm caterpillars predicted the severity of the coming winter. Owls were signs of sickness or death to come.

Most importantly, animals meant food. Grouse, quail, and wild turkey, bear and deer, woodchuck, squirrel, rabbit, and for some (but not all) opossum, were enthusiastically pursued with rifle, trap, and hound. For most men, and some women, hunting was both vocation and avocation. It brought life-giving food to the table, but was also recreation and a means of proving one's bravery and skill. A mountaineer's vacation, when the crops were "laid by" in late

summer, often consisted of a week or two of hunting in the high country wilds.

Preventing "varmints" from killing livestock and eating crops was half the job of farming. Bears, and in the early days, gray wolves and mountain lions, sometimes killed sheep on the mountain meadows where they summered. Raccoons and bears loved corn. A fox or weasel might kill every chicken you owned in one night. A bear determined enough to break into the springhouse, or worse, the meat house, could cause a family to go hungry.

When former residents, now in their 80s and 90s, talk about their childhoods in the Great Smoky Mountains, a closeness to nature is obvious. Allie Maples, a member of a long-prominent family in the Gatlinburg area, remembered, "We children in the Sugarlands had so much fun outdoors. We would play up and down the rivers, jumping rock to rock…"

Charlie Palmer of Cataloochee recalled, "they was raspberries and strawberries and June apples and all sorts of fruit, and it was more like living in the Gaden of Eden than anyting else I can think of."

Of course there was work, too. Nearly from the time a child could walk, he or she had a list of chores to complete. Children milked cows, fed chickens and pigs, gathered eggs, hoed weeds, picked bugs off plants in the vegetable garden, swept porches and yards, picked berries and gathered nuts, shucked corn, carried buckets of water from the spring, toted firewood, carried corn to the mill, washed dishes, and plowed fields. And then there was school.

It is obvious that education was important to the families of the Great Smokies because bringing schooling to the mountains took tremendous

The Beech Grove School in Cataloochee Valley was built in 1903. This schoolhouse, with its worn wooden desks and slate blackboard, was sometimes in session only a few months of the year, depending on funding. Students learned the basics, including reading, writing, and arithmetic.

Sorghum cane was fed by hand into two large rollers mounted near the top of a cane mill. The wooden sweep attached to the mill transferred power from a horse or mule hitched to it, turning the rollers, and squeezing the sap from the sorghum stalks.

Sorghum molasses was a much-prized "sweetning" in the early days. Autumn molasses-making was a festive occasion, drawing neighbors from miles around in the cooperative processing work.

commitment and effort. Throughout most of the 19th century, when a mountain community wanted a school, they built it themselves. Such was the case with Little Greenbrier School, which still stands just a short walk or drive from Metcalf Bottoms Picnic Area. The great tulip trees that form the walls were cut, hewn, and notched by the parents of the children who would attend. The teacher was hired, housed, and paid by the same. During lean years, when cash for the teacher's salary was short, school might only last for six to eight weeks, usually during January and February, when there were the fewest chores to do on the farm. And yes, some children did walk three miles to school each way, some of them barefoot, even when the ground glittered with new snow. Group photos of Little Greenbrier School pupils reveal that childhood obesity was not a problem at the time.

Though not all mountain families were large, those with 10 to 12 children were not all that unusual. In winter, kids snuggled under thick quilts, three or four to a mattress (contrast that with today's suburban gold standard of a separate bedroom for every child). Sadly, death was not nearly as infrequent a visitor to children as it is today. A trip to any of the hundreds of graveyards in the Smokies will verify this. Records show that over 50 percent of those who died during bad years were under 21, many of them infants. Randolph Shields, a resident of Cades Cove, recalled that all farm work had to cease during serious epidemics because everyone was consumed with caring for the sick, making coffins, and mourning the deceased.

Even though families were spread out from one another and transportation choices were foot, horse, or mule, socializing was a cornerstone of 19th-century life in the Great Smoky Mountains. Not surprisingly, it mostly revolved around work. Hog butchering was most efficient when more than one family was involved, both to share the labor and the spoils. Shucking 5,000 ears of corn was a lot more fun when there were a dozen or so of your closest neighbors around to help and maybe a jug of moonshine waiting at the bottom of the pile. After which there was nothing to prevent some fiddling and guitar playing, and a huge meal of fried chicken, corn bread, pickled vegetables, and stack cake for dessert.

Sorghum molasses-making was perhaps the most interesting annual work. It was accomplished in the fall, after the heat was gone and each Indian summer day brought richer color to the maple trees on the mountain and the apples in the orchard. Though just about everybody grew their own sorghum cane (which resembles tall, stout corn), not everybody owned their own mill and furnace. Cooperation made the whole process sweeter.

Families liked to squeeze their cane very soon after it was cut. The mill was powered by a horse or mule tethered to a long wooden sweep. As the animal plodded around in circles, the sweep turned the rollers on the mill, which looks something like an old-fashion clothes wringer. A person sat at the mill, ducking the sweep, and feeding the sorghum cane, stalk by stalk, through the rollers.

The resulting green juice was strained into a barrel that was carried to a wood-burning furnace built of stone. Atop the furnace sat a large, metal, chambered evaporator pan. As the fire was carefully tended, a consortium of experienced molasses-makers stirred the thickening concoction and moved it from chamber to chamber as it matured. Any lapse in vigilance could scorch the molasses and ruin the whole year's effort.

Finally, when the molasses reached its syrupy zenith, someone pulled the plug from the bottom of the tray and filled jar after jar with the perfect complement to corn bread and the secret ingredient in the world's best cookies, pies, and candies.

There was probably some fun on mill day, too. The big custom mills, like Mingus Mill at Oconaluftee, did most of their business on certain days of the week, often Saturday. Men and boys rode in on horseback, a sack of corn straddling the front of the saddle. If they were regular customers, the miller knew just how finely ground the family preferred their cornmeal.

As the farmers waited for the corn to be made into meal, there was time to talk and catch up on the news from different ends of the valley: births, deaths, marriages, good deeds, thefts, murders, and bear hunts. During good weather it must have been pleasant, for water-powered gristmills are magical places. No smoke billows from smokestacks and no engines screech. There is only the sound of water pouring from the millrace, the murmur of the nearby stream, the creak of turning wheels and gears, and the hum of the whirring stones. The warm meal you carried home would be hot corn bread in the morning.

As it did almost everywhere else across America, the pastoral era of self-reliant agrarians and close-knit rural communities drew to a close in the Smoky Mountains. Industry and mechanization came to the Smokies at the tail end of the 19th century, most prominently in the form of the great commercial timber boom, from the mid 1890s to 1939. Many

people changed from growing most of what they ate and wore to buying these staples with their wages. For better or for worse, life in the Smokies rapidly became more like life everywhere else.

Yet Great Smoky Mountains National Park preserves a slice of the history of the hardy mountain farm family during the dangerous and exhilarating days of the mid 1800s. You can see and touch a piece of it in the stone piles, the chimneys, the walls of log homes, and the beautifully maintained gristmills. The rest you need to imagine for yourself.

Blacksmiths were in great demand in earlier days, especially since horses and mules needed shoeing every couple of months. The tools of the blacksmith's trade included an anvil, billows, tongs, and a hammer.

Besides horseshoes, blacksmiths produced a variety of useful items for the farm and household, including plows, axes, and nails.

This massive log barn is part of the Mountain Farm Museum adjacent to the park's Oconaluftee Visitor Center. The museum has brought together a collection of buildings from throughout Great Smoky Mountains National Park. Besides the barn, the museum includes a farmhouse, springhouse, apple house, blacksmith shop, smokehouse, and chicken house.

As its name suggests, a springhouse was built to protect a family's source of clean, fresh water. Usually located some distance from a dwelling, springhouses like this one at the Caldwell Place also provided cool storage for perishable food such as milk, eggs, and butter.

Mill and Forge creeks provide the water for Cable Mill, which still grinds corn into cornmeal. The millstones and much of the structure are original.

The Cataloochee Valley once included a prosperous farm community. Today only a few structures remain, including this barn at the Caldwell Place.

A footbridge crossing Cataloochee Creek leads visitors to the Caldwell Place. This white frame house with blue trim was built by Hiram Caldwell and his family early in the 20th century. The house features shingled gables, weatherboarding, and interior paneling.

A large overhang on either side of a cantilever barn provided some shelter for farm equipment and for animals that were not kept inside in stalls. Farm animals frequently included cows, hogs, sheep, and chickens.

Smokehouses like this one at the Tipton Place stored salted and smoked meats. Pork from an annual hog killing was the most commonly smoked meat. Mountain families also ate beef, poultry, and wild game.

Walking the Noah "Bud" Ogle nature trail offers an excellent opportunity for viewing wildflowers. Visitors will also find this original log home, barn, and tub mill built by Noah and his wife Cindy, who began farming 400 acres here in 1879.

The rich bottom land in Cades Cove provided some of the best ground for planting in this part of the Smokies. Located between Cades Cove and Little River Valley, Rich Mountain, seen here looming above the fog, is home to a number of caves.

Mingus Mill is one of two regularly operating gristmills in Great Smoky Mountains National Park. Using a turbine that is powered by Mingus Creek, the mill ground corn and wheat. Built in 1886, the mill is now operated by the National Park Service from mid-March through November.

Water to power Cable Mill flows from the creek into a containment pond, then through the millrace, into the flume, and finally fills the more than forty buckets of the waterwheel. Of the four mills that remain within Great Smoky Mountains National Park, only Cable and Mingus Mills still operate on a regular schedule.

Family tub mills were widespread, but could only crank out a bushel or so of corn per day. This tub mill on Roaring Fork Motor Nature Trail has two circular stones, one above the other. One stone is attached to a shaft, which is turned by power from a horizontal waterwheel.

Located on the eastern bank of the West Prong of the Little Pigeon River, the Old Mill in Pigeon Forge, Tennessee, has been in continuous operation since 1830, when William Love damned the river and began construction.

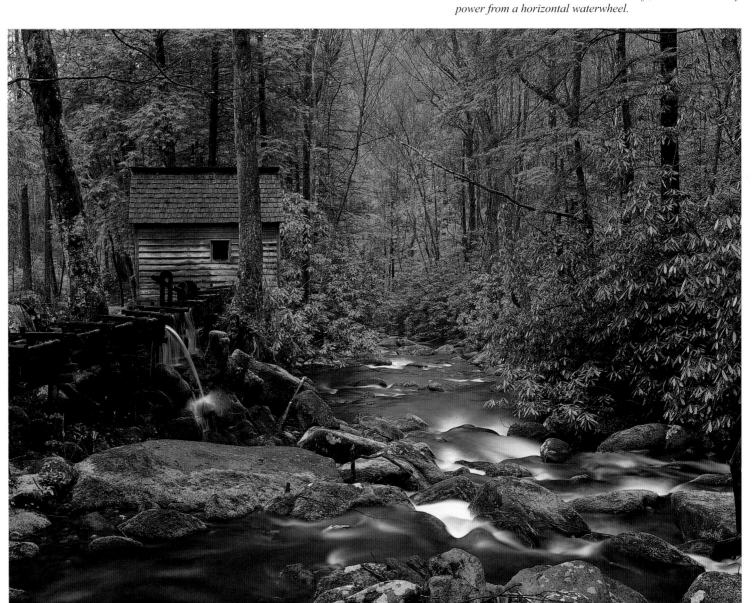

Rays of sunlight illuminate a barn in Cades Cove.

George Washington "Carter" Shields purchased this Cades Cove cabin in 1910 and lived here through 1921. It is a lovely place to visit in the spring, when the surrounding dogwood trees bloom.

John and Luraney Oliver were the first Euro-American people to settle in this area of the Smokies. Their log house is typical of many of the time, with small windows, a stone chimney, and wooden shingles. Split rail "worm" fences were easy to disassemble, move, and then reassemble where needed.

A log building served the Methodist congregation here until this frame-style church was built in 1902 by John D. McCampbell.

There are over 100 cemeteries in Great Smoky Mountains National Park, many of them small family plots. The Primitive Baptist Church cemetery has over 200 graves, including those of some of the Cove's first permanent residents—Olivers, Cables, and Shields.

About the Photographer

For over 20 years Adam Jones has practiced his craft and today is a widely recognized nature photographer whose work is widely published in posters, greeting cards, magazines, billboards, textbooks, calendars, national ads, and annual reports for major corporations. Recognized in 1995 as the BBC Wildlife Photographer of the Year for the "In Praise of Plants" category, his book credits include: *Kentucky River Palisades* (Westcliffe), *Kentucky* (Compass American Guides), and *Dr. Thomas Walker and the Wilderness Road*. A native Kentuckian, he is deeply devoted to the Great Smoky Mountains.

About the Author

Steve Kemp is also the author of *Smoky Mountain Impressions*, *Great Smoky Mountains: Simply Beautiful*, and *Trees of the Smokies* and has written articles for *Outdoor Life*, *Outside*, *National Parks*, *Outdoor Photographer*, and the Discovery Channel guidebook series. He worked as a seasonal park ranger in Yellowstone and Denali national parks and has been employed by Great Smoky Mountains Association as a writer, editor, and Interpretive Products Director since 1987.